Beyond

Greens
and
Cornbread

Beyond Greens and Cornbread

Reflections on African American Christian Identity

Diane Givens Moffett

JUDSON PRESS
Valley Forge

Beyond Greens and Cornbread:
Reflections on African American Christian Identity
© 2001 by Judson Press, Valley Forge, PA 19482-0851
All rights reserved.

Bible quotations in this volume are from the following versions:

The Holy Bible, King James Version (KJV).

The New King James Version (NKJV). Copyright © 1972, 1984 by Thomas Nelson Inc.

HOLY BIBLE: *New International Version* (NIV), copyright © 1973, 1978, 1984. Used by permission of Zondervan Bible Publishers.

The New Revised Standard Version of the Bible (NRSV), copyright © 1989 by the Division of Christian Education of the National Council of the Churches of Christ in the United States of America. Used by permission. All rights reserved.

Library of Congress Cataloging-in-Publication Data
Moffet, Diane Givens.
     Beyond greens and cornbread : reflections on African American Christian identity / Diane Givens Moffett.
          p. cm.
     ISBN 0-8170-1417-9 (pbk. : alk. paper)
     1. African Americans—Religious life—Poetry. 2. Christian poetry, American. I. Title.
     PS3613.O59 B49 2002
     811'.6—dc21   2001038783

Printed in Canada

07 06 05 04 03 02 01

10 9 8 7 6 5 4 3 2 1

In memory of my music teacher,
Mrs. Lora Toombs Scott,
who not only taught me to play and sing,
but who exposed me to the great black poets
and showed me how to speak the written word.

To my grandmother,
Mrs. Willie Mae Jessica Pope,
who shared with me the power of God
and the beauty of the Christian faith.

And to the men, women, youth, and children
of Elmwood United Presbyterian Church,
who share their lives with me
and inspire me to write and preach.

To you I am grateful.

— Contents —

Foreword by Jeremiah A. Wright Jr.   ix
Acknowledgments   xiii
Introduction   xv

1. To Each One a Gift   1
2. Counterpoint   5
3. Working the Ground of Life   10
4. Beyond Greens and Cornbread   15
5. An African American Narrative   17
6. When Did You Last Dream?   24
7. What's Inside   29
8. Beautiful Brown Babies   32
9. Calling All Sisters!   35
10. In Celebration of African American Fathers   38
11. A Charge to Listen   40
12. Forsaken   42
13. Finishing It   45
14. "And Learn of Me . . ."   47
15. Up Against a Mountain   49

16. Choices 51

17. Rising Storms 53

18. Claiming the "I Am" 56

19. Mother Sophia 59

20. Faith? 61

21. The Call 64

22. How Can I Be a Woman,
If You Won't Be a Man? 67

23. Mother's Prayer 69

24. Praise 72

25. The Way Home 74

Foreword

In one of Dr. Walter Brueggemann's monographs on the biblical prophets, he coined the powerful phrase, "And finally comes the poet!" Dr. Brueggemann argues that, after the statesmen, after the official representatives of the government and the "status quo," and after all the "spin experts" in the employ of the government, there finally comes the poet. In other words, he asserts, the true prophet of God is a poet.

The one who is truly a prophet, the one who truly "forth tells" the mind of God and the heart of God is, in fact, not just a preacher. The imagery which that man or woman of God uses is poetic imagery. That prophet-preacher is, in essence, a poet.

This definition of the prophet as poet has several levels of meaning. When you hear or read the prophet's words, each reading or hearing yields an entirely new set of messages. That is poetry at its finest. That is God's awesome way of speaking to God's people.

Brueggemann's words become flesh in the writing of Rev. Dr. Diane Givens Moffett. Rev. Moffett is truly God's prophet-poet! She not only writes the Word of God in poetic form. She also speaks to the heart of God's people in an awesome and powerful manner. As the persons called by God to be prophets in the Old Testament spoke from their particular cultural-specific hermeneutic, so does Rev. Moffett.

She writes as an African American woman. She writes as a wife. She writes as a mother. She writes as a musician. Her sermonic poems are written from the vantage point of an artist whose inner eye sees the beauty, the power, and the depth of the African American experience and its interconnectedness with the heart, the mind, and the will of God!

The end result is not only a unique genre of poetic sermons. The end result is a window into the soul of black America, into the soul of the black church, and into the soul of African American men and women throughout history who found hope in Christ Jesus and who refused to give up!

Persons of all races and ethnicities can look through the window that Diane Givens Moffett has constructed and see the pain, the power, the joy, the sorrow, the hurts, and the hearts of Africans who have lived in the North American Diaspora for four hundred years. The practice of chattel slavery in its West African manifestation is one of the ugliest experiences in human history.

Six million Jews were lost in Hitler's Holocaust. More than 100 million Africans were lost in the *Ma'afa* of the

West African slave trade. From that ugly experience, however, has come some of the most beautiful music every created in human history—the African American spirituals. Rev. Moffett's poetic sermons are cut from the same cloth as those spirituals. They open a window that enables the reader or hearer to feel the experience of having been born a descendent of those Africans who were enslaved.

The poems in this volume not only instruct and inspire. They also inform and challenge. Like the preached word of God, these written words strike deep within the spirits of those who hear them and read them to pull out the best that God has placed within each of God's creations. They touch the head and the heart, but they go deeper than that.

As a preacher-poet, Rev. Moffett helps us hear the voice of God in a new key through her writings. She helps us hear the echoes of grace as they reverberate from the jangling discord of the horrors of slavery, segregation, Jim Crow, and apartheid American style. God's voice and God's victory are sweeter than all the bitterness of those experiences combined, and Diane Givens Moffett helps us to hear that voice and its whispers of mercy blowing through the centuries, across the bows of the eighteenth-century slave ships and into the segregated black communities of the twenty-first century.

The *ruach* of God that brooded over the soul of Rev. Moffett in creating this work now blows gently and insistently upon the spirit of the reader and creates a new being. You cannot read these poems and come away untouched, unchanged, or unmoved. An encounter with the Spirit of God as it breathes through Diane's writings will create a new you, and you will be blessed forever because of the way that God has blessed her.

Share these poems with your family. Share them with your friends. Share them with persons you care about, and thank God for the gift that the Spirit has breathed into Rev. Moffett, because God's gift to her has blessed and will bless all who read this awesome work.

Dr. Jeremiah A. Wright Jr.
Trinity United Church of Christ
Chicago, Illinois

—Acknowledgments—

I want to thank Judson Press for daring to do something new and publish a book of "sermonic poems." I am blessed by their decision and encouraged by their willingness to take a chance on this new writer. Special thanks to Randy Frame who read the first draft of my work and was impressed enough to pass it on to other editors. I am also grateful to the entire staff who helped with all the details associated with publishing such a work, and particularly to Victoria McGoey, who demonstrated tremendous patience with the numerous questions I posed to her. And finally, my thanks to Rebecca Irwin-Diehl, whose superb editing skills helped to clarify and strengthen my thoughts.

My appreciation of family grows with my years. I thank God for constant encouragement from my parents, Lawrence and Vivian Givens, and from my siblings, Jackie Wagner, Julaine Smith, and Christopher Givens, and their families. Truly, you bless me! And to my immediate family,

I can't say enough about their support of my ministry and the work I do. Perhaps because they are musicians and artists in their own right, they sacrificed much to make the creative process easier. To Mondre, my husband, and to Eustacia, Jessica, and Kayla, my daughters, thank you. Special kudos to Eustacia, who read the manuscript and always assured me, "Your stuff is tight."

I want to also acknowledge my colleague and friend, Rev. Robert N. Burkins, senior pastor of Elmwood United Presbyterian Church, and the entire congregation there, for being such great people of God and for inspiring me in my journey of faith. Thanks, also, to Dr. Jeremiah A. Wright Jr., pastor of Trinity United Church of Christ in Chicago, Illinois, for encouraging me in this project. I trust that you will find meaning and inspiration from the work in this book.

Finally, I want to thank God for depositing within me the gift of creativity. Many of these poems emerged from sermon writing, pouring through me unannounced. Others came after careful reflection on Scripture and after reflection on plain old living. Whatever the case, to God is the glory for allowing me to put on paper what I see in mind's eye.

— Introduction —

Since before the days of Lucy Terry (1724–1821), the first recognized African American poet, African Americans have used poetry as a literary genre to capture the experience of being black in white America. Poetry is an excellent tool of expression. Its various forms have a unique way of capturing the inner thoughts and psyche of a person, helping us to smell, taste, hear, and feel the terrain of our humanity. In our preaching, in our storytelling, in our singing—from the spirituals to the blues—the poetic images, metaphors, and symbols take center stage, making our journey come alive in our own minds and in the minds of others. Through the various messages of the written word, our hopes and dreams, our virtues and vices, our aspirations and inspirations are made known, aiding us in our journey of faith.

I grew up memorizing and reciting the works of such great African American poets as Langston Hughes, James

Weldon Johnson, and Paul Laurence Dunbar. Poetry, like song, has become a part of me. When writing and preaching, I feel it spill over into my presentation and I let it flow in the tradition of African American orators who know how to paint a sermon and make you feel, touch, and experience their words as your own.

Beyond Greens and Cornbread was written primarily to be a tool of inspiration for its readers. The primary purpose of the book is to affirm our identity as African American Christians; to illuminate some of the thoughts, challenges, and feelings that come out of the African American Christian experience; and to inspire the reader to embrace the challenges and gift of life.

The title of this volume was carefully selected and carries three underlying meanings. The first is a challenge to readers to look beyond the outward signs and symbols of African American culture and to discover the centrality of Christ in the history and heritage of African Americans. Several poems, including "An African American Narrative," make reference to our journey from the shores of slavery into the ocean of freedom, making particular note of the faithfulness of God and of God's activity in the lives of people of African descent. Through poetic expression readers may learn how God's spirit has worked and continues to work in the lives of African Americans.

The second meaning in the title is an invitation for readers to ponder the story and contemplate the plight of African Americans in order to gain deeper understanding of the blessings and burdens associated with the color of our skin and with our culture and our heritage. Poems such as "Beautiful Brown Babies," "Choices," and "Faith" express the twofold predicament faced by African Americans. *Beyond Greens and Cornbread* calls us to develop an effectual faith that supplies the mechanism to deal with the positive and negative forces in our existence.

The third meaning, that these reflections are an invitation to move beyond the physical food of greens and cornbread to the spiritual food of God's Word, is critically important because it is this soul food that will supply the spiritual nutrients needed for African Americans to be faithful to our calling. This book, in fact, is an attempt for me personally to be faithful to my own calling.

In writing this collection, I have been aware of the scope of my poetic offering. The many voices present within the African Diaspora make it impossible for me to represent the entire race. Thus I clearly understand that the poems collected here are the interpretation of life through my particular lens, written from my unique perspective as an African American preacher woman, wife, and mother, living in the United States within a particular social, cultural, economic, and political context. They are my attempt to be faithful to what God has deposited within me.

Many of the poems that follow have been excerpted from full-blown sermons that speak of faith as it is applied in the African American context. Although written primarily to an African American audience, the reflections have been written in such a way that one of any ethnic background may glean meaning from them and the issues they raise. Thus, the works may be classified under the three broad categories of *affirmation, aspiration,* and *inspiration.*

A Scripture quote prefaces each work, providing the reader with a biblical backdrop for the message. It is helpful to note the Scripture before reading the sermon, but it is not necessary. The Scriptures are there to guide the reader in understanding the soil from which the poem grew.

The forms of the poems vary and include narrative, verse, simile, and rhyme. Some have patterns; others are "free form." The message determines the style just as form follows function.

May you be richly blessed in reading, as I was blessed in creating, *Beyond Greens and Cornbread.*

—1—

To Each One a Gift

There are different kinds of gifts,
but the same Spirit. . . . Now to each
one the manifestation of the Spirit is
given for the common good.

1 Corinthians 12:4,7, NIV

More abundant than blue skies that grace the earth.
More lavish than fresh air breathed at birth.
More generous than water that flows from the seas.
More plentiful than sunlight piercing the trees.
Sweeter than melodies humming birds sing.
Lovelier than Autumn, Winter, or Spring.
More beautiful than diamonds, gold, and things.
Giver of life,
Blessings you bring.

Resourceful and creative,
Manifold and rich,
The Spirit gives to each a gift.

Men and women of African descent—
Black, brown, and beige with a cinnamon tint,
Uniquely designed and shaped from above,
Filled with majesty, riches, and love—
Mine out the gifts embedded in you.
Seek not to own the oppressor's view.
No one can take your position and place.
Try as they may, they'll end in disgrace.
You have buried deep within
A treasure to share, a pure, precious gem . . .

Resourceful and creative,
Manifold and rich,
The Spirit gives to each a gift.

There is no best, bad, or left out.
The body is a unit, many parts about.
All are valued.
All are equipped.
All are special.
All are sent—
To share God's blessings,
To be God's script.

Resourceful and creative,
Manifold and rich,
The Spirit gives to each a gift.

Eye should never say to hand—
"I don't have a need for you!"
Without a hand, what's a body to do?
Nor should the head say to the toe,
"I don't like you. You must go!"
For each part has its use, you see.
Abolish the thought,
"They're better than me."
To do God's work,
We all must be fit—
Ready,
Able,
Competent,
Equipped.

Resourceful and creative,
Manifold and rich,
The Spirit gives to each a gift.

Men and women of African descent—
Black, brown, and beige with a cinnamon tint.
Together God's people we're called to be,
Moving in the rhythm of ministry.
A variety of service,
A multitude of gifts—
Inscribed by God
In the Holy Writ.

In light of our being,
In light of our call,
I ask the question
And pose it to all:
What are your gifts?
And how will you use them
To bless our race and further God's kingdom?

**Resourceful and creative,
Manifold and rich,
The Spirit gives to each a gift.**

—2—

Counterpoint

God is love.

1 John 4:16, NIV

Love.
Before God,
Preachers,
And packed church pews filled with anxious onlookers,
Couples vow to fulfill this word.
But do many people know what it means to
Really love and be loved in return?
To care and be cared for in return,
To know and be known in return,
To feel and be felt in return,
To accept and be accepted in return,
Without hesitation, explanation, or condemnation?

God is LOVE.

We place it with romance and mystery,
White lace and promises spoken out loud,
Secrets whispered in the dark,
In a moment of passion that passes—
Moving on,
Storming forward,
Oblivious to the wreckage wrought,
To the people and places who were
Damaged by a deceptive experience,
If only for a moment.

God is LOVE.

We package it with sex.
We sell it in magazines and on billboards,
In airports and train stations,
In liquor stores and grocery markets,
In newspaper articles and advertisements for
Cars, toothpaste, perfume, and drink.
We exploit this most precious commodity,
Making it a tool of manipulation
Rather than a instrument of healing.

God is LOVE.

We use and abuse it.
In its name we force young men and women
To make war and spill blood
On behalf of country and race,
To kill and to steal,
To hate those who are different,

To destroy the "miss-fits"—
Persons who force us to test our assumptions,
Shift our thinking,
Break the paradigms of life that we
So easily cling to.

God is LOVE.

We have perverted it,
Twisted it,
Messed it up and mixed it up.
And the greatest offense?
The promotion of the counterfeit version
To our young people
(By adults with more cash than wisdom)
In music videos,
In gangster rap,
In film and T.V. shows.
No wonder many young black males
Measure their manhood from the waist down,
Instead of from the head up.
No wonder many young black females
Are babies having babies,
Giving birth before growing up.

God is LOVE.

We have missed the mark.
We have marred the meaning.
We have distorted the truth.
We have concocted a lie.

More than romance and mystery,
More than sexual expression,
More than a reason to buy what we buy,
More than an excuse to do what we want to do,
More than a tool of manipulation . . .

God is LOVE.

The very essence of love—
Healing
Holding
Caring
Comforting
Encouraging
Enlightening
Restoring
Reconciling
Saving . . .

God is LOVE.

God shares true love—
Pure love,
Authentic love.
Love poured into a human mold—
A yielded cup,
An open vessel.
Love found in a person—
No, not in "your" man or woman,
Not in your "sweet thing," "sugar daddy,"
    or "darling, darling baby"—

But in Jesus Christ.
He is Love Divine—
God's love,
With flesh on it.

God is LOVE.

Although we may not know
We are known by God.
Although we may not care
We are cared for by God.
Although we may not feel
We are felt by God.
Although we may not accept
We are accepted by God.
Without hesitation, explanation, or condemnation.

God is LOVE.

Available for "whosoever,"
Above, beyond, greater than anything we can imagine.
Infinite
Endless
Timeless
Boundless

GOD is LOVE.

—3—

Working the Ground of Life

But the fruit of the Spirit is love, joy,
peace, patience, kindness, goodness,
faithfulness, gentleness and self-control.

Galatians 5:22, NIV

Piercing the skies of heaven
The eyes of God look down upon the earth—
Surveying the soil of human souls,
Searching the ground of human hearts,
Roaming the landscape of human nature,
Seeking a place to plant the fruit of the Spirit.

Piercing the skies of heaven
The eyes of God look down upon the earth—
Finding rough and rocky earth,
Discovering stones and pebbles in the dirt,
Spying thorns and thistles in the mire.

Break up the hard clay!
Transform our nature!
Work the ground of our life!

Dig, God!
  Dig hard,
    Dig long,
      Dig deep,
        Dig wide!

Dig with the shovel of your hands—
Dig down to the bottom,
Dig down to the core,
Dig down to the essence of our being.
Dig down to the point of our problems—
Racism,
  Sexism,
    Ageism.
The "isms" we hate
But can't escape—
Pounds of dirt stacked against us,
Poison spawned within us,
Producing
  Self-hate,
    Self-doubt,
      Self-degradation.

Break up the hard clay!
Transform our nature!
Work the ground of our life!

Dig, Lord!
  Dig far,
    Dig near,
      Dig big,
        Dig well!

Dig down and strip us of stones and pebbles.
Dig down and free us of rocks and rough earth.
Dig down and rid us of thorns and thistles.
Dig up the stuff buried so long
We hardly notice it anymore.
Dig up the muck and mud that keep us
Struggling in the swamp of self-destruction.
Dig until we discover the beauty of our blackness.
Dig until we love ourselves as we love others.

Break up the hard clay!
Transform our nature!
Work the ground of our life!

Dig, Savior!
  Dig up,
    Dig in,
      Dig through,
        Dig great!
Root out,
  Weed out,
    Rake out,
      Pull out—

Vines that choke the seed of your Word . . .
Expose idolatry—
   Dependence on psychics,
     Addictions to astrology,
       Trust in manna and the state of the stock market.
Arrest our search for you
   In crystals and New Age charms,
     In the occult and modern-day sorcery,
      In the predictions of false prophets,
And the backward wisdom of a world gone wild.

Break up the hard clay!
Transform our nature!
Work the ground of our life!

Dig, Jesus!
   Dig quick,
     Dig calm,
      Dig broad,
       Dig large!

Uncover dry soil.
Make it fruitful once again.
Pour water into the arid places of our lives.
Saturate the cracked ground of our being.
Seep through the parched plains of our existence.
Heal the ache in our head,
   The wound in our heart,
     The hole in our soul.

Break up the hard clay!
Transform our nature!
Work the ground of our life!

Remind us that you are active in the world—
In the bedroom and in the board room,
In public and in private,
Seeing our virtues and vices.

Prune us back as the gardener who seeks better fruit.
Till our soil until it is fertile and rich.
Till us until we become soft clay in your hands.
Till us until we shift under the power of your presence.

Build us up.
Make us stand on higher ground,
To be people who bear the fruit of the Spirit—
Love
Joy
Peace
Patience
Kindness
Goodness
Faithfulness
Gentleness
And self-control.

—4—

Beyond Greens and Cornbread

As the deer pants for streams of waters,
so my soul pants for you, O God.

Psalm 42:1, NIV

Out of the darkness
Pushed from a mother's warm, watery womb
Gasping for air and desperate for breath . . .
The search begins at birth,
The search for somebody—
Someone
Some meaning
Something
Beyond ourselves.

Innately,
Intuitively,
Instinctively,

We are compelled to ponder—
The reason for our being,
The intent of our birth,
The purpose of our coming . . .
Beyond ourselves,
    our traditions,
        our culture,
            our community.

Beyond the clay form that houses our spirit,
Beyond nappy hair, thick lips, and broad noses,
Beyond our color, culture, and condition,
Beyond our race, creed, and confessions,
Beyond greens and cornbread,
    mashed potatoes and fried chicken,
Beyond our Sunday-go-to-meeting religion.

The soul reaches for union with God—
For oneness with the Spirit,
For dust and divinity,
The human and the holy
To finally embrace,
Marry,
And fulfill
The calling of God.

—5—

An African American Narrative

This calls for patient endurance and
faithfulness on the part of the saints.

Revelation 13:10b, NIV

Proud Africans were my foreparents.
Born in a rich, dark, fertile land,
A land sparkling with precious jewels
    and valuable stones.
Born in a land where the sun shines bright,
Coloring the skin of its people in a rainbow
    of black hues—
        Suntan
            Copper
                Bronze
                    Mahogany
                        Chocolate.

Proud Africans were my foreparents.
Endowed with thick lips, thick hair, and thick bones,
Endowed with great intellect, great spirit, and great
    creativity,
Alive with feet to dance, hips to swing, and bodies to
Sway to the sound of instruments celebrating the
    moments of life—
Celebrating birth
    Death
        Manhood
            Womanhood
                Marriage.
Celebrating the rhythm of life,
The beat of the drum,
The music of our Maker.

Proud Africans were my foreparents.
Proud were they until the day
Our community was betrayed—
Betrayed by people who looked like us—
Victim of clanship and rivalry.
Betrayed—and sold.
Sold into the hands of white oppressors who enslaved us.
Sold like animals for economic gain.
Sold like objects to be owned and controlled.
Sold like Jesus for 30 shekels of silver.
Sold.

Proud Africans were my foreparents.
Forced to sail across the Atlantic Ocean,
Packed as human cargo in the hull of ships.
Some committed suicide.
Some lost their minds.
Many died—
Most held on to life
Allowing sorrow to fuel a revolution of
Hope . . .
   Hope for freedom.
      Hope for a new life.
         Hope for the future of humanity.
            Hope in God!

Proud Africans were my foreparents.
Hope was hushed by the reality of slavery.
It was a season to mourn . . .
   Stripped of family ties
   Stripped of names
   Stripped of culture
   Stripped of native tongue.
Slavery.
Treble-cleft wails rise from the bottom of emptied souls.
Slavery.
The icy, cold winter of life with no signs of spring.
Slavery.
The pride of my African foreparents was diluted,
Bathed in salty tears and the dark pool of grief.

White oppressors taught us to hate ourselves.
Could anything good be black?
Our dark skin and thick hair,
Our thick lips and thick bodies,
Our pidgin English—
All bore witness to their bigoted belief in our inferiority.
They waged war for the submission of our humanity.
The weapons?
  Violence
    Hatred
      Abuse.
Women, raped.
Men, slaughtered.
Infants, snatched from their mother's nursing breast.
Families, divided and dealt like playing cards.
Children watched and learned.
And Scripture justified the horror?
  Cursed be Canaan!
  Cursed be Ham!
We screamed.
We shouted.
We prayed to a silent God . . .
A God who seemed not to speak.
And in the name of religion, slavery continued,
Unabated for more than 200 years.

But, truth smashed to the ground will rise again.
Their White Christ became our Black Jesus.
God spoke.

We listened and we learned
That we would rise.
By God's hand we would rise.
Like Jesus, we did rise!

Rise like the morning sun.
Rise like the Easter star.
Rise like yeast in the dough of bread.

Rise with our leaders—
      Nat Turner
    Denmark Vesey
  Marcus Garvey
Frederick Douglass.
Rise with our leaders—
      Mary McLeod Bethune
    Sojourner Truth
  Lucy Craft Laney
Ida B. Wells.

Proud African Americans were my foreparents.
Renewed by the Spirit and anointed in power,
One people out of many tribes,
Shaped and formed by the Potter—
A determined people
  A persistent people
    A stubborn people
      A strong people
        A visionary people.
Hope rose up.
The revolution began.

Proud African Americans were my foreparents.
A glimpse of deliverance came in 1863—
Slavery died.
We celebrated, "Juneteenth style."
But the black man's hallelujah
Was the white man's heartache.
The slavery's death was not readily accepted.
Many grieved its passing
And resisted.
The revolution had just begun.

The Ku Klux Klan flourished.
Segregation thrived.
   Hatred
     Rejection
       Lynchings
         Jim Crow laws.
The Thirteenth Amendment changed the Constitution
But not the heart of a racist nation.
The revolution had just begun.

Proud African Americans were my foreparents.
Fighting the revolution they prepared
For the long battle ahead—
Armed with the weapon of prayer,
Armed with the defense of the gospel,
Armed with a vision of God,
Armed with a purpose in mind,
Armed with the strength of the black church.

An army prepared for the revolution.
"Attention!"
   Martin Luther King Jr. stood up and preached.
      Coretta Scott King stood up and prayed.
         Malcom X stood up and taught.
            Betty Shabazz stood up and tutored.
               Rosa Parks stood up for her right to sit down.
The revolution had just begun.

Proud African Americans were my foreparents.
By the hand of God and the sweat of human flesh
The dream of freedom is becoming a reality.
The legacy of African Americans is etched
   in the foundation of history.
Lest we forget the road they have traveled,
Lest we think we have arrived here alone,
Lest we betray our community,
Discover the power and wisdom in knowing
The vision God has for us—
Knowing how we may accomplish it,
Knowing . . .

Proud were our foreparents.
They are calling us,
   Wooing us,
      Imploring us—
Stay in the fight.
Hope in God.
And hold on!

—6—

When Did You Last Dream?

Where there is no vision,
the people perish.

Proverbs 29:18, KJV

When did you last dream?
When did you last sit down for a moment
And see yourself, your family, your community
Making changes?
Breaking down the dividing walls in society,
Causing the raw materials of hatred, injustice,
    and oppression to
Burst open—
Burst open and crash,
Crumbling into dust,
Blown away by the Wind—
Blowing . . .
And ushering in a new era of freedom and progress.

When did you last dream?
When did you last feel passion about some subject—?
Passion about a Scripture you read,
Passion about a living word preached,
Passion about some issue that pierced your heart
    till it made you bleed
And you saw in your blood the blood of others,
And you refused to stand among the willing wounded . . .
You moved.
You moved for help.
You moved toward healing.
You moved because you knew that if you did not move,
If you stood still,
You would die—
And with you many others.

When did you last dream?
When did you last sense
    (like Mary, the mother of God)
The Holy Spirit working through
    Your mouth,
        Your ears,
            Your hands,
                Your feet,
Causing you to
Conceive something you did not create,
Say something you did not plan,
Hear something you did not know,
Write something you did not author?

When did you last dream?
Dream for the wholeness of God's creation,
Dream for the health of African people,
Dream for the vibrancy of the Christian faith,
Dream for the soundness of the community.

When did you last dream?
Dream until your heart ached,
Dream until your soul hurt,
Dream until your thoughts consumed you,
Dream until you said,
"I must arise and work!
   Work like I've never worked before,
   Labor like I've never labored before,
   Respond like I've never responded until
     this present moment."

When did you last dream?
You dreamed and you knew that dreams come true.
You dreamed and afterward said,
   "All things are possible with God."
You dreamed and said, "It shall be so."
You dreamed and said, "I will work to make it happen."

When did you last dream?
Has life been so bad that it has kept you from dreaming?
Have the demands of living drained your inspiration?
Has imagination been choked out of you?
Have you found yourself living like a dried-up fig tree?

When were you last watered—
Really watered?
When did you last know yourself to be
   in the presence of the holy—
And you could not leave?
And you would not leave,
Because your cup was empty
And deep
And the water made your parched flesh come alive again,
And the water just kept coming—
Flowing
   Filling you with ecstasy
      Flowing in you
         And flowing out of you.
You were drenched.
You could not leave
For you knew in that moment God was reaffirming
The Spirit's presence in you.
And you came to yourself,
And you were satisfied . . .
Anointed . . .
And you began to dream.

Where are the dreamers?
Where there are no dreams, there is no passion.
Where there is no passion, there is no energy.
Where there is no energy, possibility yields to doubt,
And doubt to complacency.
Where there is no dream, life is void of joy and hope.

Living becomes the management of people
and circumstances.

My God, where are the dreamers?
Give us the dreamers!
Give us those with imagination and creativity—
Those with drive and dogged determination,
Those with intellect and wisdom,
Those who are inspired,
Those who refuse to give up their dreams.

My God, where are the dreamers?

—7—

What's Inside

But you are a chosen people,
a royal priesthood, a holy nation,
a people belonging to God,
that you may declare the praises of
him who called you out of darkness
into his wonderful light.

1 Peter 2:9, NIV

Hid beneath the outer She
My face, my smile, my cheeks and nose,
Behind the makeup that I show,
The Fashion Fair that makes me glow,
My strut that takes me to and fro,
The words I say, the air I display . . .

Inside of me
Underneath my feminine flare,
The hair I style,
The clothes I wear,
The scent I flaunt,
The things I share . . .

Inside of me
Deeper than my dark-hued flesh,
Under the garb of my "womanist" dress,
Hidden beneath pure, private parts.

Who am I?
Who are you, Sister?

Hid beneath the outer He
Behind your face of strength and pride,
Your thinking, piercing, wondering eyes,
The way you walk, the pace you take,
The chivalrous charm that makes you rate.

Inside of you
Underneath your masculine flare,
Your fine mustache, your beard and hair,
Your dress, your mien, the cologne you wear.
The impact you have, the self you share.

Inside of you
Buried in your shadowed soul,
Beyond black pride that makes you whole,
Hidden in cloaked humanity . . .

Who are you, Brother?
Who are we?

What's inside
These bold, dark frames?
Created from ashy clay,
Painted black,
Placed in the Potter's kiln,
Made brilliant.
Shaped by the Artist's hand,
Formed complete,
Designed to reflect the Light,
The Imago Dei . . .

Beautiful Brown Babies

Train up children in the right way,
and when old, they will not stray.

Proverbs 22:6, NRSV

Joy splashes over me
On this day and in this hour
Of prayerful reflection . . .
Thoughts rewinding,
Mind running back,
Taking me to savory moments
When life broke through the narrow canal
And I gave birth—
Anxiously
Painfully
Willingly
Gleefully—
To beautiful brown babies . . .

Pain pulsates within me
On this day and in this moment
Of mournful reflection . . .
Thoughts emerging,
Mind running fast,
Taking me to staggering scenes
Where life breaks through the narrow canal
And we give birth—
Lovingly
Quietly
Bitterly
Tearfully—
To beautiful brown babies . . .

Beautiful brown babies placed in our care.
Beautiful brown babies,
Weak,
Frail,
And bare.

Beautiful brown babies we fail to feed.
Beautiful brown babies,
Starve,
Cry,
In need.

Beautiful brown babies dying from AIDS.
Beautiful brown babies,
Left alone,
Adrift,
On the waves.

Beautiful brown babies female and male.
Beautiful brown babies
In slave ship jails.

Beautiful brown babies paying the price.
Beautiful brown babies,
Gaining the wages
In shame and strife.

Beautiful brown babies, learn to be strong.
Beautiful brown babies, learn right from wrong.
Beautiful brown babies we must show
The path of faith,
The way to grow.

Beautiful brown babies, God's gift to us.
Beautiful brown babies, skin soft to the touch.
Beautiful brown babies, may you be infused
With strength from God and wisdom to choose
The One who is able to give you true life,
The Mother of mothers,
Jesus, the Christ.

Calling All Sisters!

"If you knew the gift of God and who
it is that asks you for a drink, you
would have asked him and he would
have given you living water."

John 4:10, NIV

Calling All Sisters!
Sisters looking for living water,
Liquid love that satisfies the panting heart.
Old sisters
Young sisters
Big sisters
Small sisters
Fat sisters
Thin sisters
Short sisters
Tall sisters
Light sisters
Dark sisters
Come see a man who sees behind the face you front.

Get to know a man whose concern
    for you transcends your
Age
Size
Weight
Height
And color.

Calling All Sisters!
Sisters searching for surpassing wealth,
Sacred bonds that secure the peace of the restless spirit.
Poor sisters
Rich sisters
Smart sisters
Dumb sisters
Come get a drink from the one who knows your longing.
Come invest in one whose investment
    in you exceeds your
Poverty
Wealth
Intellect
And foolishness.

Calling All Sisters!
Sisters waiting for the "perfect man,"
Come know the divine one who can fill the well
    dug in your soul.
Sisters in the suburbs
Sisters in the city

Sisters in the country
Sisters in the town
Sisters in the factory
Sisters in blue collars
Sisters in white collars
Sisters who are hurting
Sisters who are helping
Sisters who are crawling
Sisters who are climbing
Come meet a man who knows more about you
    than you know of yourself.
Come to the one who meets you where you
Live
Work
Ache
Hope
And dream.

Come and meet a man who can meet all your needs!
Come to the well that never runs dry!
Come to the fountain
    that will not cease to flow!
Come drink from the river
    that is bursting with new life!
Come quench your thirst
    with the waters of salvation!
Come taste and see that God is good!

—10—

In Celebration of African American Fathers

"The Lord has sought out a man
after his own heart and appointed him
leader of his people. . . ."

1 Samuel 13:14, NIV

To the man who loves his bride and wife
After the honeymoon is over
And the years have slipped away
And the hair grows gray
And the love never fades . . .

To the man who cares for his children
When they fall into the abyss
And when they rise in their prime
And as the seasons pass
And the joy comes.

To the man who looks with sparkling eyes
When grandchildren come to visit
And they giggle, play, and fight
And run through the house
And peace follows them.

To the man who honors his own dark face,
And when morning comes and work calls,
He rises up
And provides for family
And prays for God's blessing
And hope rises with him.

To the man who leads his family clan
When Sunday comes and church bells ring
And worship starts with prayer
And singing God's praises
And all are gathered there.

To this man—
Wives
Children
Grandchildren
And family—
Sing songs of celebration
And shout cries of thanksgiving!

—11—

A Charge to Listen

Hear what the LORD says to you . . .

Jeremiah 10:1, NIV

Listen—
For the voice of God speaks through the sacred page,
Uttering inspiration for souls of ebony hue.

Listen for bold words shouting across the centuries,
Timeless and eternal truths
That will not fade with fashion, trends,
    and technology—
Truth sent to pronounce promises of God to you,
Truth that severs the ropes that bind
    black prisoners of thought.

Listen for soft words spoken beneath
    the hush of silence,
Buried within texts that lose all
But a few who stop to linger,
Wooed by the beauty of phrases
That live in the depths of wisdom,
Wooed by promises
To deliver dark souls and encourage the spirit.

Listen for provocative words,
Strong, melodic statements that play in your mind,
Enhancing your perception of the reality
You encounter in this time and place—
A reality that moves you to search God's Word
And to discover the end of all your searching is in
Arriving where you began and knowing that place
For the first time.

Listen—
For the Spirit of God speaks through
    the sacred script of life . . .
Declaring
    Liberation!
        Redemption!
            Salvation!
To you.

—12—

Forsaken

"My God, my God,
why have you forsaken me?"

Matthew 27:46, NIV

Forsaken.
Abandoned.
Deserted.
Renounced.
Left behind.
Walked on and walked out on.
Left to die . . .
To suffer alone with himself,
Through himself,
All by himself.
No warm-blooded, kindhearted, Spirit-filled
Relative or friend
To touch his hands and whisper sweet comforts in his ear.

No one to wipe his feverish brow
Or to offer him a cup of cool water.
No one—
Not even God himself—
To bless him,
Pray for him,
Speak the Word to him—
To anchor his soul
So he can sail through the death waters
That will soon wash over him.
No one to be with him in his final hour.
My God, my God—why?

Forsaken.
Captured.
Enslaved.
Tortured.
Disenfranchised.
Held back.
Segregated.
Isolated.
Hated.
Discriminated against.
Unemployed.
Colored by negative self-images.
Made the blame for society's ills.
No compassion or respect shown for
    human life of African descent.
My God, my God—why?

Who will bring relief from the beatings
   and lynchings in Caesar's court?
Who will wipe the racist filth from
   the victim's feverish brow?
Who will heal the hearts and souls of black folk?
Who will fight for the future of Africa's Diaspora?

The Forsaken.

Jesus was—
So you and I do not have to be.

—13—

Finishing It

When he had received the drink,
Jesus said, "It is finished."

John 19:30, NIV

"It is finished."
Words uttered through cracked lips
   and a parched tongue—
Words uttered by one thirsting for truth
   and dying for righteousness—
Words of resolution and resignation—
Words of surrender and cessation—
Words of submission and subjection—
Words uttered after all of this—
"It is finished."

After turning himself into himself and disappearing
   in Mary's womb,
After being born an infant king in a Bethlehem stable,

After being baptized in the Jordan
　　and anointed in the Spirit,
After wrestling in the wilderness
　　and praying in the valley,
After calling twelve disciples
　　and sending twelve apostles,
After preaching in temples
　　and teaching on mountain tops,
After healing broken bodies
　　and rescuing shipwrecked souls,
After afflicting the comfortable
　　and comforting the afflicted,
After showing us the way, the truth, and the life,
After presenting the new humanity
　　made possible in him—
Jesus lets go.

"It is finished."
After the task is fulfilled,
After the work is accomplished,
After the assignment is completed,
After the labor is done,
After you have done all you can do,
After you have presented yourself—
Bold, dark, and lovely,
A living sacrifice—
Let go!
Let the Finisher finish it.

—14—

"And Learn of Me..."

"Come unto me, all ye that labour and are
heavy laden, and I will give you rest. Take
my yoke upon you, and learn of me . . . "

Matthew 11:28–29, KJV

Do not assume you know me well.
Like an artichoke, the layers of my being are many.
Peel them back.
Unwrap the outer mystique.
Discover life's source.
Come into the inner chambers of my heart.
Learn of me.

Do not assume you know yourself.
Like a rose, many petals unfurl to reveal the heart of you.
Breathe in your scent—

American flowers from African seed.
Grow in me, and I'll grow in you.
Plant roots in rich soil.
Watch life come forth.
Learn of me.

Do not take my presence for granted
Like the color purple, I am to be appreciated.
Give me time.
Read my Word—
Let my Word read you.
Honor me as I honor you.
Bathe in my presence; relax in my Spirit.
Learn of me.

Do not take your presence for granted.
Like a quilt, life's blanket is created from many pieces.
Be yourself.
Weave yourself through this world's complex fabric.
Do not be torn by the wear of despair.
Trust the Designer; rest in the Maker.
Learn of me.

—15—

Up Against a Mountain

"Truly I tell you, if you say to this mountain,
'Be taken up and thrown into the sea,'
and if you do not doubt in your heart,
but believe that what you say will come
to pass, it will be done for you."

Mark 11:23, NRSV

Have you ever been up against a mountain?
Blocked by bureaucratic systems
That perpetuate racism and breed bigotry?
Blocked by institutions
That seem indifferent to human suffering?
Blocked by the refusal,
    The denial,
      The arrogance,
And the inability of the "powers that be"
To acknowledge the problem
    and seek a sensible solution?

Have you ever been up against a mountain?
Burdened by the maintenance of those structures
In the church and in the world
That no longer suit our needs
Or address our concerns
But that we are bound to keep
Because no one is bold enough
   Or bad enough
      Or brilliant enough
         Or courageous enough
To break out of the box and
Do a new thing?

Have you ever been up against a mountain?
Barred by a barrier that doesn't seem to move?
Stuck in a situation that has not progressed?
Tied to a plight that teases the soul and makes you wonder
If you'll ever see the other side of through?

Have you ever been up against a mountain?
Smack dab in the middle of circumstances
You know you need to change
But the deck is stacked against you,
The difficulties are many,
The obstacles are high,
The impediments tall,
And you sometimes think—
Transformation is impossible.
Conversion is just a dream.

What do *you* do when you are up against a mountain?

—16—

Choices

The time is fulfilled,
and the kingdom of God is at hand;
repent ye, and believe the gospel.

Mark 1:15, KJV

There comes a moment in life when you are forced
    to make some tough decisions—
Decisions that will impact your destiny
    and determine your future,
Decisions that display your character, countenance,
    and constitution,
Decisions that reveal your nature, your substance,
    the essence of your being.

There comes a moment in life when you must
    make some crucial choices—
Choices that will affect your direction
    and chart your tomorrows,
Choices that unveil your sense, substance, and soul,
Choices that expose your heart, your spirit,
    the state of your humanity.

There comes a moment in life when you must
    make some resolutions—
Resolutions that will disclose your purpose
    and define your mission,
Resolutions that lay bare your faith, feelings, and fancies,
Resolutions that divulge your fire, your desires,
    the wheels that drive your existence.

When the season is present,
When the period has come,
When the "time is fulfilled,"
You must kiss destiny
And romance chance.
You must confront the challenge.
You must deal with the problem.
You can no longer
Avoid the circumstance,
Deny the issue,
Evade the subject, or
Ignore the question.

You must make a choice.
You must speak.
You must decide.
What will it be, black man, black woman?
What will it be?

—17—

Rising Storms

Before very long, a wind of hurricane
force, called the "northeaster,"
swept down from the island.
The ship was caught by the storm . . .

Acts 27:14-15, NIV

Breaking into our lives,
Disrupting patterns,
Upsetting scales that weigh in the balance,
Crashing down on our existence,
Beating on our boats and blowing in our faces—
With no regard to age, race, or gender,
With no concern for who we are,
Where we are, or
What we've been through.
This bold and fierce intruder whips into our territory
With violent tremors and whistling winds,

Humming eerie sounds that signal trouble has arrived,
Up front and in our face.
Yes—
Storms do rise in our lives.

We can try and play it safe by
    Never venturing into uncharted waters.
We can dock our boats near the shores of safety.
We can scurry and seek shelter—
But storms have a way of finding you.
Troubles and trials know how to seek you out.
They barge in surely and steadily,
Causing you to lose your compass
And compelling you through
Frustrating and frivolous obstacle courses.

Storms.
We can't dismiss them.
We can't run from them.
We're forced to face them—
Fight them,
Defeat them,
Or give in and let them rock us,
Wreck us,
And toss us into the raging seas of despair.
Yes—
Storms will rise in our lives.

We know about storms—
We left Africa's shores in a storm.
But while we may be able to predict the feverish forecast,
Wisdom tells us that we cannot control the weather.
Storms seem to have their own thoughts . . .
So, too, must we have our thoughts.

Think on the One who can calm the storm.
Look to the One who can walk on the water.
Cling to the Lifeguard who can rescue you.
Catch hold of the Preserver tossed for your safety.
And present yourself before the One
Who keeps us from drowning.

— 18 —

Claiming the "I Am"

"I tell you the truth," Jesus answered,
"before Abraham was born, I am."

John 9:58, NIV

I AM.
Beyond bearing witness to one's existential reality
These two words are pregnant with potential and power.
When I say, "I am,"
I engage in
Self-defining,
Self-talk,
Conversation,
Expression,
Dialogue between the Creator and the created.

I AM.

Such words are like apples of gold in a setting of silver,

Words that remind me that the power of the universe

is at my disposal.

I am a child of the Most High God.

I AM.

I know I am,

For I see God's power in my still, black soul.

I AM.

The waters of trouble, tragedy, and tribulation

Cannot put out the fire that burns within my being.

I AM.

The winds of adversity, hardship, and pain

May bend but won't break me.

I AM.

I've traveled rough roads

And been in crooked places.

I've been through the valley

And camped in the wilderness.

I've trekked up the mountain

And rested on the peak.

I've danced with the Spirit

And sat with the Son.

Through it all, I have learned,

Through it all, I can share,

God doesn't put on me that which I can't bear.

I AM.
My lover may leave me,
My marriage may end,
And my children may desert me.
My health may be waning,
My money might be dwindling,
And my job may be moving.
Yet I still declare . . . I am.

I AM
Mystically
   Miraculously
      Majestically
Created by a
Mighty
   Magnificent
      Matchless
God who
Shares spirit and life
And so
I AM.

—19—

Mother Sophia

Wisdom has built her house.

Proverbs 9:1, NIV

Mother Sophia,
Your hand rocks the cradle of the dark child
Gift to African people,
To all people.

You give and receive.
You bear and share.
You germinate and cultivate.
You till and nurture.
You sow and reap.
You bring life and give life.
You appreciate your gender
    and respect your femininity.

You know the power and pleasure
   of having been created female.
You are Wisdom—
A living translation of the Divine!

Wisdom,
Your husband sings!
Your offspring celebrate!
You have built your house well.

—20—

Faith?

"Why could not we cast it out?"

Mark 9:28, KJV

Why?
Why can not we cast it out?
This is the private question of puzzled disciples.
It is the question mumbled in prayer
When the negative forces of life overwhelm us,
Refusing to relinquish their hold.

Why?
Why can not we cast it out?
Illness and disease,
   Sorrow and grief,
      Depression and despair

That eat up our insides, leaving us
Empty,
Hollow.

Why?
Why can not we cast it out?
Abusive relationships,
   Illicit affairs,
      Dried-up marriages
That lure us into self-made prisons, leaving us
Chained,
Broken.

Why?
Why can not we cast it out?
The fear of failure,
   The obsession of greed,
      The drive for success
That make people pawns, leaving us
Stranded,
Unemployed.

Why?
Why can not we cast it out?
The putrid rot of racism,
   The sour smell of sexism,
      The foul stench of classism,
         The bitter pungency of ageism

That divide the human family into sections—

Black	White
Male	Female
Poor	Rich
Young	Old

Leaving us
> Separated,
Destroyed.

Why?
Why can not we cast it out?

Run	it out.
Walk	it out.
Shout	it out.
Think	it out.
Read	it out.
Pray	it out.
Fast	it out.
Keep	it out.

Faith flows and generates energy
> through partnership with God.
The union of Creator and creature produces power.
Together, with God we can
Cast it out!

—21—

The Call

"Whom shall I send,
and who will go for us?"

Isaiah 6:8, NRSV

Be still.
God is calling.

Early in the morning when moonlight fades
And the sun hugs the sky with its brilliant light.
At high noon when the day's half spent,
And light casts a shadow through office windows.
In the still dark night after cool winds
And sweet zephyrs have melted the scorching heat.

In the midst of the hustle and bustle,
The aggravation and frustration,
The game and gambles of life.

A voice can be heard,
Speaking to listeners

Who pause to hear the stirring message—
Be still.
God is calling.

The call wakes and shakes,
The call humbles and humors,
The call amazes and mystifies,
The call convicts and challenges
The receiver.

The call is persistent and consistent,
Piercing and pulsating,
Demanding a response—
Like a phone that won't stop ringing,
A beeper that won't stop beeping,
E-mails that just keep coming.

God speaks and says,
"I have my eyes on little ole you.
I've got something for you to do,
A mission to accomplish,
A task to complete,
A goal to fulfill,
A work to achieve."

Come
Move
To higher heights
   deeper depths.

Come
Move
From the ordinary
    to the extraordinary.
Come
Move
From the cosmetic
    to the core of your being.
Come
Move
From spectator to leader
In my world.

Be still.
God is calling.

—22—

How Can I Be a Woman, If You Won't Be a Man?

Husbands love your wives . . .

Ephesians 5:25, NRSV

When you stay out late at night
And you treat it rather light.
When you fail to talk to me
And pretend that I don't see.
When you act so unconcerned
And think I can't discern
I'm not in your plans...
How can I be a woman, if you won't be a man?

When the monthly bills are due
And you seldom help me through.
When you say that work is long
And you sing the poor man's song.

When you seldom take a stand
And provide with able hands
For our needy clan . . .
How can I be a woman, if you won't be a man?

When you drop me off at church
And leave me in the lurch.
When you will not take the time
To renew and change your mind.
When you never feed your soul
And your heart grows hard and cold
But you reach for my warm hand . . .
How can I be a woman, if you won't be a man?

Mother's Prayer

The prayer of the righteous
is powerful and effective.

James 5:16, NRSV

Late at night when the sky is dark
And the moon shines
Like a brand new nickel
And the stars sparkle
Like a brand new diamond,
And the earth sleeps
Like a brand new baby . . .

A mother prays
On bended knees
Turned black
By the friction of human skin,

Prostrated to plead the plight of
Her children,
Her family,
Her world,
Herself.

From her center a river pours,
Filling eyes
With salty water that
Drops buckets of tears for
Guidance,
Protection,
Trust,
Hope.

And when the sacred moment ends
She rises
To join the sleeping crew
Still at rest.

Early in the morning when the sky is blue
And the sun shines
Like a brand new penny
And the clouds kiss the sky
Like a brand new love
And the earth wakes
On a brand new day . . .

A mother sings a brand new song,
Confident in the knowledge that
Her children
Her family
Her world
Herself
Are cradled in the arms
Of the Mother of All.

—24—

Praise

Let everything that has breath
praise the Lord!

Psalm 150:6, NKJV

Zoom, Zim, Zaat!
The organ hums,
The sound swells up
And fills the sanctuary corridors.
My body vibrates,
My flesh tingles,
My insides wake up.

Clang, Cling, Crash!
The symbols sing,
The drums roll out
And shake the aisles of hallowed halls.
My toes tap the rhythm,
My shoulders move,
My hands clap a beat.

Ping, Pang, Pound!
The piano plays,
The harmonies spring forth
And hit the air of sacred space.
My ears soak up the sound,
My spirit soars,
My eyes drip salt.

Squee, Squat, Squam!
The trumpet talks,
The notes dance free
And speak in a coded language.
My memory jolts,
My soul knows,
My temple rejoices.

I know the music,
The music knows me.
Music of my past.
Music of my present.
Music of my future.
Unrehearsed,
Improvised,
Bold,
Beautiful,
Black . . .
Music of praise.

—25—

The Way Home

"For the Son of Man came
to seek out and save the lost."

Luke 19:10, NRSV

Roads rise and bend.
Streets twist and turn.
We get lost.

Lost from ourselves
And from our God.
Lost in
Titles,
   tenure,
      trades.
We mask insecurities by thinking
What we have determines who we are.
We get lost.

Lost from ourselves
And from our God.
Lost in
Money,
   mores,
      matter.
We hide anxieties by thinking
What we need is more than what we have.
We get lost.

Lost from ourselves
And from our God.
Lost in
Loving,
   living,
      longing.
We disguise ruthless drive by thinking
What we have now is not what we want.
We get lost.

Lost from ourselves
And from our God
Lost in
Color,
   creeds,
      conflict.
We conceal racist lies by thinking
Who we are is not who we want to be.
We get lost.

We get lost from ourselves
And from our God.
We glance,
But we do not grasp.
We look,
But we do not understand.
We see,
But we do not perceive.

God is searching for you.
God is calling for me.
God is seeking the lost,
Seeking to find us
For ourselves
And for our God,
Seeking to show us the way home.